BLUFF YOUR WAY IN
ADVERTISING

NIGEL FOSTER

D0202119

RR

RAVETTE BOOKS

Published by Ravette Books Limited
Egmont House
8 Clifford Street
London W1X 1RB
(071) 734 0221

First printed 1988
Reprinted 1991
Revised 1992
Reprinted 1993

Series Editor – Anne Tauté

Cover design – Jim Wire
Printing & binding – Cox & Wyman Ltd.
Production – Oval Projects Ltd.

The Bluffer's Guides series is based
on an original idea by Peter Wolfe.

An Oval Project
for Ravette Books Ltd.,
an Egmont company.

CONTENTS

WHAT IS ADVERTISING?

As all bluffers know, everyone has something to sell. Even if it is only a point of view.

Advertising is simply a way of selling something, anything, in the most effective method possible. There is no great mystery to it and not really all that much science – despite the efforts of various people to turn it into one, largely to justify their expense accounts.

A little light-hearted fun can be had in pointing out that the advertising business itself is often confused as to what it actually does, *viz*:

'Advertising is the origination and/or communication of ideas about the products in order to motivate consumers towards purchase.'   David Bernstein

'Advertising presents the most persuasive possible selling message to the right prospects for the product or service at the lowest possible cost.'
                         Institute of Practitioners in Advertising

'Advertising isn't a science. It's persuasion. And persuasion is an art.'   Bill Bernbach

In many countries, thought not the USA, selling is seen as something that is not quite nice. Thus advertising often goes to extraordinary lengths to distance itself from the image of the used-car and double-glazing salesmen. This explains, in part, why many television commercials are extremely witty and well made, but do not actually sell anything. Except, of course, the skills of the people who make them.

Advertising Theories

Since advertising is essentially to do with human behaviour, it can only be an inexact practice at best, and usually something of a gamble. This has not stopped its gurus from producing interminable theories as to what makes good advertising. These come and go as fast as the ads themselves leaving just the memory of their mnemonics – for instance:

AIDA: The advertisement must capture Attention, arouse Interest and make consumers Desire the product, so stimulating the Action of rushing out and buying it. (Or **AIDCA**, which goes one better and requires that the ad has to Convince consumers they need the product.)

VIPS: The ad has to be Visible; to Identify the product; to Promise some benefit, and to do this with Simplicity.

However, nothing quite beats the maxim coined by Samuel Johnson:

'Promise, large promise, is the soul of an advertisement.'

Attempts to apply some sort of scientific discipline to the business mean that advertising is now an acceptable business to be involved in. Academics have been presented with a whole new subject to write about, which means the industry is now full of people who should really be analysing flow rates and sedimentation in municipal sewerage farms.

Nevertheless, theories have one major and vital function: they enable the agency to reassure the client that it really does know what it's doing.

THE AGENCY

Agency Philosophy

It should be understood that the advertising agency's intention is not, as might be first thought, to make as much money as possible in as short a time as practical. In fact, agency philosophy behind the intention describes:

a) what the agency believes good advertising is;

b) what the agency believes a good product is;

c) how the agency believes good advertising should be created;

d) how the agency believes it should conduct its business;

e) what the agency believes makes an agency so much better than its rivals;

all of which is designed to help the agency make as much money as possible in as short a time as practical.

Many agencies are very proud of their philosophies. Much time is spent polishing them so that the client can see a reflection of his own business beliefs. The very word 'philosophy' suggests that:

− many intelligent, altruistic people have spent long hours thinking Big Thoughts;

− ad agencies are inherently noble, as is advertising itself;

− a specific ad agency might just hold the secret of how to sell widgets which are identical to all other widgets, but cost twice as much.

7

Many successful agencies have been built around a single 'philosophical' belief. In this way they resemble certain fundamentalist religions. You should be able to defend at least one such belief, preferably with a straight face.

For example, you might like to extol the virtues of the **USP** or Unique Selling Proposition. This holds that to be successful any product must be demonstrably different from its competitors, and that the advertising should present its unique attribute in such a way that the consumer will choose it, rather than any other.

There are always flaws in building an agency around any belief. In the USP one, for instance, the problem is that:

- it is often easier to invent an advertising USP than to produce an actual product that possesses one

- consumers rarely behave rationally

- any product and its advertising that majors on a single USP (classically, only one USP is allowed at a time) becomes decidedly dreary.

Point out that the USP theory was around for a long time before it appeared in any agency philosophy. Claude Hopkins, the legendary copywriter working at the beginning of the century, used it all the time. He just called it selling.

In real terms, all philosophies are one of three types:

- The agency knows best.

- The consumer knows best.

- The client knows best.

Agencies holding the first belief are likely to be known for their brilliant creativity. Agencies holding the second are known for the size and thoroughness of their marketing department. Agencies holding the third just stick around, year after year.

Whatever views they proclaim, deep down all advertising people believe that they know best, and that advertising would be a wonderful job if it wasn't for the **client**, the **consumer** and the **Advertising Standards Authority**.

Agency Politics

Producing good advertising is all about politics. You will recognise that, just as politicians slither towards decisions that will upset the least amount of people, so agencies try and produce good advertising that will not upset:·

- their client
- other clients
- their bankers
- their creatives
- any larger agency who may be thinking of a take-over.

As a result, life inside an agency is best compared to life within a medieval court, or Rome under Nero, or Hollywood before the Academy Awards. It may be true that you cannot please all the people all the time, but it is the business of advertising agencies to try.

Anyone wishing to survive should soon develop all the skills of a modern-day Machiavelli. Otherwise those barbed comments passed in fashionable wine bars could be aimed at your own back.

Nor will you realise that you have been professionally assassinated until you discover that your office has been 'temporarily' relocated to a small cupboard, your company car changes overnight from a Porsche to an Astra; the receptionist looks at you with mingled pity and contempt when you come to work in the morning, and you are given an account to work on that the agency should have resigned as unprofitable years ago.

If this happens, it is almost invariably too late. Somewhere you have blundered. Possibly you have made the cardinal error of stabbing so many others in the back, that you clean forgot to watch out for your own.

But take heart, there are a number of basic rules for survival. Follow them diligently. You may never be headhunted for an astronomical salary, you may never win any awards, the press may never run an archly sycophantic article about you, but at least you will hold your own.

Rules for Survival

1. Find out who really holds the reins of power in the agency. Remember that it is not always the most obvious person. For example, an otherwise modest and unassuming art director (almost a contradiction in terms) can turn out to be the nephew of the chairman of the bank that owns most of the agency's shares.

2. Pin-point the various factions (on the board or otherwise) and figure out where the person who recruited you stands. If he or she is on the losing, or weaker, side, make it known that you are quite prepared to help in their demise – not for reasons of personal ambition, but solely for the good of the agency, the product and the client.

3. Work out as soon as possible where your own discipline stands within the agency, and never mind what you were told when they hired you. If, for example, you are a highly proficient planner, it may well be that your job is essentially cosmetic: the agency wants to be seen to be taking planning seriously, while in truth the creative, media, marketing or account handling disciplines will continue to hold sway. If this is the case, begin looking for a new job.

4. Ascertain whether the management has finally decided what the agency stands for and believes it. If so, become an immediate and devoted convert to the company line.

5. Discover where the real strengths of the agency lie, as opposed to the claimed ones. It may well be that an agency publicly priding itself on its creativity, actually holds its clients because of its excellent media buying. Or because it is superb at providing clients with seats for Wimbledon, Twickenham, or Covent Garden. Then dress to suit the dominant culture.

6. Establish the major outside influences on the agency, i.e. who or what adds to the incipient paranoia. These could be city analysts, the trade press, business school professors or Patric Walker's horoscope. Learn all you can about them, and suggest (but never claim outright) a personal relationship.

7. Identify those individuals who are the unofficial leaders within the agency; those who act as advisers to the senior executives. And who also often know where all the bodies are buried.

8. Never make an enemy out of a secretary or receptionist, or even the lowly go-for in production. It is more dangerous than being better dressed than the managing director.

9. Remember that many have made the mistake of getting close to their opposite number on the client side, thinking that this will help protect their job. And so it will, until the opposite number is promoted, or fired, or hired by your own agency.

Agency People

Advertising prides itself on being a people business. The astute will have noticed that there are very few businesses that are not to do with people. However it is best to follow this party line wholeheartedly. Aside from anything else, it makes for a wonderful excuse whenever something goes disastrously wrong, *viz*:

"Yes, we lost the account because the art director tried to eat the client's pet Chihuahua, but this is a people business."

"I'm sorry that the chemistry between the client and me just isn't right, but it can't always be right, this is a people business." (This, when you alone have been responsible for spending twice as much on an advertisement as the client agreed.)

Certainly it behoves all bluffers to know the nature of the beasts they work with.

Account Executives

Account executives or account handlers (a suitably positive term) were once known as contact people because they were in day to day contact with the client and are now known more affectionately, or derisively, as 'suits'. Sometimes even as 'empty suits'. It is their sad lot in life to explain agency thinking to the client and client thinking to the agency. Not surprisingly, many develop split personalities (both of which will be paranoid).

Account executives have to know many, many things – marketing, media, planning and even what 'creatives' do (though in this they are not alone: lots of other people would like to know exactly what creatives do, not least those who pay their wages).

What account executives think they do:

– Mastermind brilliant campaigns.

– Keep the account profitable.

– Act as a focal point for all agency activity.

What they actually do:

– Praise everyone else when things go well.

– Take the blame when things go badly.

– Hide from the creative department on those rare occasions when they are genuinely needed.

– Overspend the media budget.

– Deliberately lose at golf.

– Try to set up their own agency.

How to handle:

Never make the mistake of flattering account executives. Knowing that you do not mean it, they will suspect the worst. Instead, encourage them to talk about themselves and their great successes. Account executives never admit to failures, only errors of judgement due to being "badly briefed".

Try to keep your relationship strictly on a professional level, although it is acceptable to worship the same New Zealand wine, or if the executive is female, to claim a lifelong devotion to the work of Fay Weldon.

If executives start to cause you problems, play on their paranoia. Make a show of covering up memos when they walk into your office. If you are casually chatting to the managing director when one approaches, stop deliberately until he or she walks past. Then, later, when asked what the MD was saying, be obviously evasive and avoid looking them in the eye.

If these ploys fail, you can always spread the rumour that the executive is planning to leave the agency, taking the best accounts. Aside from anything else, it will probably be true.

Creative Directors

The creative director runs the creative department, often the agency as well. Always be on the best possible terms with creative directors; when they leave to set up their own agency, they just might take you with them.

Art Directors

Art directors are in theory responsible for the visual aspect of an advertisement. In practice, art directors will direct practically anything: the campaign, the account, the commercial, the agency, the client, and the personal lives of anyone they find attractive.

No-one is quite sure why art directors believe that they are good at everything, and why they are allowed to get away with it. Rumour has it this dates from the days when the art director controlled the supply of magic markers and was the only person who could put down Letraset without tearing half the characters.

You could hold the view that the exaggerated respect with which art directors are treated is because advertising people believe that:

a) artists can draw and understand perspective

b) art directors are artists.

What they think they do:

– Produce superb advertising.

– Co-operate with all their colleagues.

– Battle bravely on despite those around them.

What they actually do:

– Insist on trying to do everything themselves.

– Reluctantly allow a small amount of copy to appear in a press ad (but only if set in six point).

– Stare moodily into space for days on end.

– Call in a freelancer when stuck for an idea.

How to handle:

Never flatter, never cajole. Treat art directors as thorough-going professionals, even if they go missing ten minutes before a full client meeting. Always give them the credit for an idea the client thought was brilliant, whoever actually thought of it.

Find out who their favourite soccer team is, and get them the occasional ticket.

Copywriters

Copywriters have the hardest job of all because everyone, from the art director to the client, 'knows' that they can write as good copy as the copywriter, but of course they have more important things to do with their time.

In theory, copywriters are responsible for all the words that appear in an advertisement, or dialogue in a commercial. They are also supposed to produce those irritating **tags** and/or **slogans** without which no ad of any kind is considered to be complete.

What they think they do:

– Produce superb advertising.

– Possess a unique insight into the client's problems.

– Write like a dream.

– Have the ability to think visually.

What they actually do:

- Spend days looking through books on great ads of the past for an idea.
- Argue marketing strategy with the account handlers.
- Drive the art director wild with suggestions for the visual treatment of an ad.
- Insist on writing the camera directions for a commercial.
- When blocked, work on their novel.

How to handle:

First try wit. If that does not work, ask for help and sound as if you mean it. Never threaten physical violence.

Planners

Once upon a time the best advertising agencies had someone who dealt with market research. Nowadays, they have planners.

Their function is still the same, they exist to:

a) confirm the creative department's hunches

b) persuade the client to spend even more money.

The only difference between today's planners and former market researchers is that they are paid a great deal more money and they are allowed to meet the client on a regular basis.

Avoid pointing out that many agencies were producing pretty good work before planners came along and that those agencies who believe strongly in planning still manage to make the most horrendous mistakes.

The truth is that planners are liked by:

- clients – because they manage to make advertising sound logical

- the agency's bankers – because they appear to have some measure of control over the creatives

- academics in business schools and universities – because here is yet another discipline in which they can claim expertise

- the trade press – because it gives them something else to write about.

Planning has been enthusiastically accepted by the advertising business because it makes the business look sound.

What they think they do:

- Input consumer preferences and attitudes to develop realistic advertising objectives.
- Establish creative parameters.
- Develop advertising strategies.

What they actually do:

– Tell the creative department how to do its job.

– Tell account handlers how to do their job.

– Hold secret meetings with the client's head of market research.

– Produce interminable sets of data (which can be used to prove anything, but which is usually used to prove how indispensable planners are).

How to handle:

If you work with an agency that earnestly believes in planning (and there are one or two around), try to sound enthusiastic about focus groups. If not, feel free to put a planner on the defensive by claiming that there is no such thing as unbiased research: that the mere fact research is being undertaken will have an affect on the findings (always good for a long argument).

Planners are often the nicest people to be found in advertising. Since it is accepted by most others in advertising that they are especially vulnerable, show your support by agreeing that they make a genuine contribution to the business.

Media Planners

In many ways the priesthood (strongly non-celibate) of the advertising agency world, media planners decide where and when an advertising campaign should appear in order to:

a) reach the correct target groups

b) maximise the client's media spend

c) show the agency in the best possible light.

Theirs is an arcane world, full of computer print outs, strange phrases, endless charts, diagrams and rating points. Be wary of media planners; they are pretty good bluffers themselves. It is they who have to explain to a client why, for example, a commercial for floor wax should appear during a late night, avant-garde chat show. (Real reason: the media planner's spouse or lover helps produce the late night, avant-garde chat show.)

What they think they do:

- Apply scientific method to the generally frenetic advertising process.
- Save the client money.
- Make the campaign a success.

What they actually do:

- Practise working their calculators blindfold.
- Learn new jargon.
- Discover new and wonderful advertising media.
- Blame media buyers if anything goes wrong.

How to handle:

Show the respect due to those who are also living on their wits. If necessary, media planners can be reduced to incoherence by changing the media brief thirty minutes before a client meeting. "Oh, sorry, weren't you told? No, it's nothing but bus cards I'm afraid... Look, come along anyway, I'm sure you can help change their minds." Alternatively, produce a campaign that demands odd sizes for the ads.

Media Buyers

This happy breed are the official wheelers and dealers of the advertising business. They are responsible for buying any and all the media (print, television, radio, cinema, etc.) that the client has agreed to. And a good deal that he has not. Media buyers are therefore the people who manage to keep the agency profitable, and use bluff as a matter of course in their dealings with media reps. A good media buyer will be able to buy space or time at a far lower rate than the official one. This is not always mentioned to clients, lest they query their media budget.

What they think they do:

– Control the advertising business.

What they actually do:

– Get taken to long liquid lunches by media reps who are desperate to unload time and space.

- Make extravagant promises.
- Forget to mention that they did not get that vital TV spot during the evening news.

How to handle:

Use tact and diplomacy. If you are lucky, you may get invited to one of those legendary entertainments that the media puts on for advertising agencies. One where everyone gets at least one glass of wine.

Receptionists

Receptionists are chosen as much for their physical charms as for their business abilities. However, they usually possess more natural abilities than the obvious ones. They can make or break an ad person's career.

What they think they do:
- Form the agency front line in the face of visits from clients, couriers, backers and bailiffs.

What they actually do:
- Know, and repeat to the favoured, all the agency gossip.
- Neglect to give messages and vital packages to people they do not like.

How to handle:

Treat with care: they have heard it all before. Remember their birthdays with flowers (but not roses if you're male, unless you want a visit from her large muscular boyfriend). Always tell her where you are going and why, remembering to be a little economical with the truth.

Secretaries

Secretaries in the agency world are rarely, if ever, actual secretaries. There are many who know as much, if not more, about what the agency is doing as the managing director and whose administrative talent, not to mention instinctive understanding of advertising itself, makes the whole agency work.

How to handle:

Treat as you would your closest colleague.

THE CLIENT

Agencies always refer to the companies they deal with as 'the client' even if several people are involved on the client's side. It is therefore impossible for an outsider to know who is being talked about, which means you can be as rude as you like about 'the client' in restaurants and pubs.

Clients fall into one of at least four categories:

1. Those who deeply distrust all advertising agencies, but cannot see any alternative.

2. Those who believe they could probably do the whole thing themselves, using freelancers and consultancies, but don't have the time.

3. Those who love advertising agencies and are only waiting to be offered a job.

4. Those who are confused by the advertising process and cling to any ad agency sensible enough to flatter their ignorance. For some reason, these are very often the ones who are offered an agency job.

Clients have varying degrees of importance. Within a large to medium sized company there will be certain functionaries concerned with advertising; within a small company there might be one person, and he or she is invariably out to lunch.

It is essential to establish which people on the client side are important. Otherwise you could spend an hour or so discussing long term strategy with someone whose main job is to make sure the company logo appears correctly on all company products.

Advertising Directors are the main client scape-goats, responsible to the Chairman and Managing Director, and sometimes the Marketing Director, if the company believes that advertising is a function of marketing, not a separate function.

Marketing Directors are unhappy talking to creatives but blossom in the presence of agency planners.

Advertising Managers may be advertising directors in all but name, and may also be those unfortunates responsible for checking the spelling on every press ad and every packet.

They are often the messengers deputed to tell the agency that the advertising director has changed his mind and wants to use outdoor advertising instead of television as originally agreed. When taking on this rôle they resemble rabbits coping bravely with a family of stoats who've moved into the same burrow.

Ad managers are supposed to be the technicians who understand what agencies mean by 'point size', 'bleed', 'RoS', etc. They deal with middle-ranking account executives and are never normally allowed anywhere near the creatives for fear of being bullied.

Assistant Advertising Managers are rarely allowed anywhere near the agency.

Brand or **Product Managers** are only found in large companies where they huddle together for warmth. They are nominally responsible for the overall performance of a particular product or brand and thus combine marketing, advertising and sales. Their true function is to believe the product they are presently handling is the best in the world.

These people will try to liaise with everyone in the agency from the Chairman down, but are usually only let loose on junior account executives whose naïve enthusiasm is equal to their own.

Assistant Brand Managers find it hard to find anyone to talk to. So if the client suddenly announces that from now on the account will be handled by a **Junior Assistant Brand Manager**, or an **Assistant Advertising Manager**, it is probably time to look for a new client. Or a new job.

Keeping the Account

There are two times when an agency formally presents work to a client:

1. When it is pitching for the account.

2. When it is trying to hold on to the account.

Presentations should always be pitched a fraction above the clients' level of comprehension, but with the implied assumption that the client understands exactly what the agency means. This is known as success by intimidation, and is central to ad agency culture.

Experienced advertising people know that anyone

can win an account. The trick lies in keeping it – long enough to make it profitable. An agency begins to lose an account from the moment it is first appointed. This may take months, years, or decades – but lose the account it will, often for totally unfair reasons. In fact always for totally unfair reasons, since it is a tenet of agency life that no client fully understands either the agency, or what the agency has achieved for its client.

This means that accounts are largely retained by pampering the client. The account executives are responsible for day to day pampering, largely in the form of **the lunch**. Many clients see the lunch as being the one bright spot in an otherwise drab world. Clients also lean on account executives for other types of solace ranging from tickets to major sporting events to brain-storming sessions in the Bahamas, and a certain 'emotional' comfort. It is often easier to simply develop a social relationship and thus become a family friend.

Occasionally the agency is blessed with a client who is intelligent, experienced, sensible and honest. This is when you should really panic, knowing that every other agency will work twice as hard to steal him from you.

When clients themselves provide a written brief – mostly when shopping around for a new agency – the brief should be ignored. However, when clients have changed the brief, usually at the last moment, there is only one response. They should always complimented on "providing us with the means of making a really significant contribution to your overall plans, and we mean that sincerely".

This gives them the impression that all those highly paid agency people cannot operate without their leadership. They need never know otherwise.

CREATING CAMPAIGNS

In the good old days, ads were created by copywriters rootling around the client's business until they found something interesting to write about, one hour before the client presentation.

In fact, not very much has changed. Everything may appear to be more scientific, but the underlying hope that an idea will emerge from hysterical confusion remains the same. No matter how many surveys, focus groups, or in depth analyses of the optimum product profile have been conducted, at some point someone will be left staring with mounting panic at a blank sheet of paper, relying on creativity, not numbers, for the answer.

A great deal of research in advertising is undertaken to discover what previously went right or wrong, so that triumphs can be repeated and disasters avoided. This may explain why so many advertising campaigns look the same, even the bad ones. It is important to appreciate that ads are created by people who are scared of losing their jobs, which adds a certain piquancy, not to mention drama, to the entire process.

Many more people now appear to be involved in creating ads and campaigns than ever before. This makes it easier to find a scapegoat if things go wrong. There is safety in numbers.

It is also true that only big agencies can attract truly big clients since:

a) many clients would be horrified to discover that their account could be as easily handled by two people and a dog (the office junior). Often a client's standing is based on the size of the agency chosen.

b) many advertising managers (clients) grow in status with the size of the agency team reputed to be working on the account

c) both sides fondly believe, that the more staff working on an account, the greater the possibility of someone coming up with a good idea.

On the other hand, there are agencies that favour a 'lean, stripped-down approach' (the industry is full of gung-ho sporting analogies). They will claim to use the bare minimum of staff on an account, all of whom, naturally, will be able to 'run with the ball'. In this situation you may take it that at the agency:

- half the existing staff are about to leave or be fired

- new staff cannot be hired because the agency chairman intends buying Mustique.

Ad campaigns used to begin with the client figuring out what needs to be sold, to whom and for how much. A fairly straightforward process that seemed to work, until everyone realised that they could demand larger salaries if it was more complicated, and so developed 'marketing'.

Agencies traditionally answered the later 'how' question – 'how to sell something that no-one wants, to people who can't afford it'. But since the marketing-led seventies, agencies have also been asked to help with the first part of the equation. They can then be held responsible if it all goes wrong.

Whatever the mechanics, the agency will always ask what is in it for them, and make sure that something is.

The Meeting

At the early stage, the agency itself will know little or nothing of what is being planned. They will know that the account team on that piece of business is looking more than usually smug. And that the planning people have begun to work behind locked doors.

Then comes the day when the account executive calls a meeting to announce the start of a new campaign. The client advertising manager may also be present, wearing a new power outfit. This meeting will also include the agency team selected to work on the project:

- creatives, looking jaded
- planners, looking eager
- media planners, looking mysterious
- (sometimes) media buyers, looking fragile.

The purpose of these meetings is to reassure everyone that the product has been fully researched, and that a viable market exists for it. No-one will actually believe this, least of all the creatives, but this is one of those quaint agency practices that has lasted through the years.

The meeting ends, in most instances, with the account director promising to give everyone their individual briefs as soon as possible. Then nothing happens for some days, often weeks.

The art director goes back to the drawing board, the copywriter to that unfinished novel, media planners return to their esoteric diagrams, and media buyers to insulting media reps. Until the day a directive appears on everyone's desk.

The Brief

No ad campaign can be said to begin until the account team has fully briefed – on paper, please – everyone else involved. The content of these briefs varies from agency to agency, and is often dependant upon how well the account person responsible can spell.

The reason why briefs often take so long to appear can be summed up in one word: fear. No-one likes to put anything in writing which can be used to damn him or her at some later date. Never mind that briefs can be amended by memo later on. Be sure that only the original brief will be remembered, and that the creative team will probably refuse to work to anything else. Unless the changes are their own idea.

Those responsible for writing initial briefs should remember to:

a) keep it as short as possible

b) keep it as non-specific as possible

c) get the client's name right.

Always ask for comments (but never suggestions) by the next day. When tackled about this deadline, state blandly that everyone should have been thinking about this project since the first meeting.

Essentially these briefs will set out the client's aims and objectives. Ignore the temptation to try and set a strategy; a strategy only becomes apparent some time after the campaign has broken, if at all.

Keeping the strategy deliberately vague will also help you shoot down everyone else's preliminary work, as in: "Yes I see what you're trying to achieve – but the client will never go for it, it's not on strategy."

When asked, murderously by the creatives, sincerely by everyone else, what exactly the strategy is, simply refer them to:

a) the first meeting, and any other meetings there may have been since;

b) various contact reports, that everyone will have lost and no-one will have bothered to read.

You can also play one department off against the other, as in: "Strategy? Well, we're waiting to see what the Creative/Planning/Media/Suits have to say about that... in the meantime, let's continue on these broad lines, okay?"

There are agencies where the strategy is developed in the very beginning; everyone understands it; everyone follows it; contact reports are read religiously; and everyone knows exactly what is happening at any particular point. There is no proof that agencies like this produce better advertising than agencies which operate in complete confusion.

The Campaign

As the development of the campaign gets under way, casual observers will note that:

- the account executives begin to have longer and longer lunches

- the planners become even more intense

- the media planners surround themselves with a laager of files and facts

- the creatives take a few days off,

- the client looks forward to the next meeting, at which he/she will:
  a) change whatever strategy exists
  b) mention casually that an approach has been made by a rival agency (but claim total loyalty to the existing one "because we know you're going to do a Great Job on this new campaign, right?")

Shortly after this, the account handlers will insist on a meeting with the creatives to discuss 'initial concepts'. This meeting will inevitably result in the creative director and managing director being called in to adjudicate.

It is out of this meeting that a clearer strategy arrives: not so much concerned with what is needed, as with what is not.

The Research

The inexperienced may well wonder what the planners tell the creatives. Essentially they will try to explain:

a) what kind of people will want to buy the product;

b) why they will want to buy it

c) how they voted in the last election.

This last is rarely, if ever, relevant, but planners like to throw in little nuggets like that from time to time.

Once upon a time consumers were categorised in

strict socio-economic groups. Actually, more economic than socio, based on the principle that while money cannot buy happiness, it can buy everything else that the agency wants to sell. Today, despite the changes it is generally agreed that:

* All consumers think of themselves as belonging to a socio-economic group at least one higher than they actually do, except for those at the very bottom.

* Buying-choices do not always have a great deal to do with how much money a person can afford to spend.

However, since the halcyon days of ABC1s, C2s and DEs ('As' driving around in Ferraris, 'Es' walking around with newspaper stuffed into the holes in their shoes), revolutionary methods of defining the consumer have emerged.

Consumers are now understood to have quite complex preferences, and clients have even been forced to admit that there may indeed be a difference between what they want to sell, and what consumers are prepared to buy.

Research is often used to establish the product's personality – even the most humble can benefit from the assignment of human attributes such as 'warm', 'friendly', 'faithful', 'cheeky'. Product, or brand, personalities are considered essential since so many products are effectively the same. Confine yourself to stating that you never met a product you weren't prepared to take home to meet the family, and try not to smirk while saying it.

Much is based on the theory that consumers:

- Do not always know why they buy something, (i.e. that they are not always aware of their innermost desires, at least, not the first time).

- Must be continually assured they have made the right choice, particularly in the face of rival advertising.

- Can be educated to develop a fierce loyalty to a specific brand or product.

Never discount research. It gives you one more reason why it was not your fault that the campaign lost the account. Unless you are responsible for the research in the first instance in which case the excuse is that creative/media did not follow the research brief. If that does not work, blame the client. If all else fails blame the agency, and take the account to a new one.

The Media Plan

The media plan will have been decided by the media planners within ten seconds of being told the budget for the new campaign.

But true professionals take their time. Media planners are nothing if not astute. They realise a simple statement at the very beginning that, say, the client needs 'x' number of spots of whatever duration on television or radio, or press ads or outdoor or direct mail, will make them sound like amateurs.

The basic question is quite simple – what is the cheapest method of selling a certain type of product to a certain type of people? Sadly, it's not that simple. All sorts of surprising factors come into play, e.g:

a) the client will insist on the reverse of that which is recommended (television campaign if you've planned for radio, or direct mail, if you recommend outdoor advertising);

b) the agency will be desperate to unload some surplus TV spots left over from a previous campaign. (This means that the planner will have to convince the client of the need to advertise to Scottish crofters at four in the morning.)

c) the creatives will have secretly sold the client a campaign using inappropriate media but which is undeniably brilliant and bound to win awards.

The reason for a media planner's charts and diagrams is not to show what should be done. They are used to forestall – or pour cold water on – anyone else's unauthorised ideas.

The Presentation

At some point, often coinciding with the account handlers joining Alcoholics Anonymous for the fourth time, the agency will produce a coherent and logical campaign. This has to be presented to the client, which is what many agencies think they do best.

It is vital to understand that presentations bring out the worst in absolutely everyone.

Clients oscillate between a total inability to make up their collective minds, and a fair impersonation of Saddam Hussein. Creatives begin enthusiastically, end morosely. Planners become nervously defiant. Media planners end up talking about concepts that Einstein would have been hard-pushed to understand.

Account executives argue fiercely for the campaign for 99 per cent of the time (especially if the creatives are present), only to capitulate in the end and admit that the client is absolutely right to reject it.

There are very few agencies that will present work they genuinely believe is absolutely correct and refuse any changes, other than the time honoured one of making the client's logo larger.

On occasions, the campaign will be presented to the client solely by the account executive, often at the client's own offices. This happens for various reasons:

a) the client likes playing God

b) the creative work was actually done by a freelance, since sworn to secrecy

c) the account handlers think this is the best way of getting their own ideas across

d) the creatives cannot be trusted to behave

e) the agency is presently talking to one of the client's main competitors and an accidental meeting of the two would be fatal.

Creatives in particular dread these presentations, feeling with some justification that they are being judged and condemned in absentia. Creatives must learn how to decipher the account executive's comments when he/she returns.

What they say:	What they mean:
The client approved in principle.	It needs a major re-work.
I fought for it as hard as I could.	I caved in immediately.
There is just one minor change.	The one thing you loved, they hated.
We're all going to have to have a re-think.	We lost the account.
The client was impressed with the visuals.	The copy has to be scrapped.
The client loved the copy.	It's time the art director changed.
I finally managed to convince the client.	The client took one look, loved it and doubled his budget for next year.
Fancy a drink after work?	I've been fired and need help getting a new job.

The Production

Provided the agency has managed to come up with a campaign the client likes, the next hurdle is producing it. There is one cardinal rule that applies between final presentations and the advertisements or commercials appearing in public: advertisers never get the final work they expected and agencies never produce the final work they intended.

One of the main reasons for this – aside from all those scintillating little afterthoughts that occur to everyone – is production cost: how much it actually costs to make commercials, or press ads or whatever. Production cost is always:

- more than the client can afford
- less than the creative department expected
- about what the account executive feared.

Major production costs are incurred with television commercials. As with a good deal of modern art, these are not so much judged by what the general public thinks of them, as by what the advertising business thinks of them. This is because the general public is not, generally, considered astute or knowledgeable enough to form a proper opinion. Agencies, and clients, do not produce television commercials for the general public. They produce them to impress each other.

Commercial concepts may be presented to the client via:

a) a storyboard, a collection of drawings giving the sequential action of the commercial. Storyboards are often more exciting than the final result.

b) animatics, a basic cartoon version.

c) scripts, which will probably show all the camera directions and feature acronyms like ECU (extreme close-up); LS (long shot); SFX (sound effects); VO (voice over), MOOZ (reverse zoom), etc.

Very few clients are capable of figuring out from a storyboard, animatic or script what the agency intends to produce. This is just as well since it will be nothing like the original concept. And the director is bound to ignore the directions written by the creative team.

Once the commercial has been agreed and cast, all is ready for the shoot itself. There is a continual fight to prevent the client from attending a shoot. Clients become panicky when they realise how much filming time is spent just standing around, all at their expense.

If the client insists on being present, this is one time when the account handler can become a true hero to his creative colleagues. It is his duty to prevent the client from interfering, or trying to date the actors – both of which are bad for business.

It is not necessary to know film jargon, except that words like 'dolly', 'brute' or 'blonde' should never be taken at face value. Anyone with a job title with which you are totally unfamiliar will probably be someone vital to the production or someone important in the union.

Even if you happen to know something about the process at hand, pretend to know nothing. This will endear you to the crew and you may be allowed to sit in a canvas chair. You may even be allowed to look through the camera.

Commercials will invariably be shot by an outside production house. Production houses calculate their costs by:

– estimating the figure for the job

– adding 30 per cent for contingencies

– adding their own profit

– doubling the result.

The agency will then add an extra 40 per cent before passing it on to the client. When confronted, agencies justify the large cost of commercials by pointing out that the expense only represents a tiny fraction of the television spend.

Given the chance, you should encourage any commercial that needs to be shot in an exotic location: everyone will love it save for the client's financial controller, but he won't be invited.

The Launch

The commercial is ready. It has been shot, edited and had all special effects added. The client's sales force has been shown the result. Their reaction will range from excited cries to a slow intake of breath and much shaking of heads.

All that remains is to get it on the air. This is often the time when the media buyer responsible suddenly changes jobs, and the account handler discovers that the promised spots have not in fact been booked; or if they have, it is at a rate far in excess of the buyer's promise, or if contracts have been signed with the relevant television companies, no-one noticed the cunning get-out clause which allows the television company to add an extra 15 per cent.

Clients, too, at this point, are fond of saying: "Look, we think it's great, you know we do, but do we really need a sixty-second commercial? Couldn't we get as much mileage out of a thirty second ad? How about editing it...?"

A sensible account executive would, at this point, take a few days off.

When the commercial, in whatever form, is finally broadcast, there only remains the post mortem. This may range from a collection of sad-faced groups drinking furtively in corners, to a fully fledged party complete with cabaret. At this time it is traditional for:

a) agency people to say what they really think of each other

b) the client (if present) to say what it really thinks of the agency

c) account executives to start talking about setting up their own agency.

CAMP FOLLOWERS

No agency could produce any type of advertising without the help of outside sources. Particularly those companies and consultancies run by a relation of the client, the agency creative director or chairman.

Photographers

These tend to specialise – in fashion, cars, pack shots or whatever. Avoid discussing the finer points of photography with photographers since they find detailed discussions about F-stops a little tedious, and you will be paying by the second for every reluctant word. Photographers like to be seen as the high-priests of their art, and hold most agency creatives in thinly veiled contempt.

Paste-up Artists

The ones who are responsible for all the fiddly aspects of putting an ad together, i.e. putting down letraset and typesetting, fitting photographs to size, etc. Whether they work in-house, or on assignment, they seem to earn an excessive amount. But many have been made redundant by computers.

Visualisers and Illustrators

These will turn the art director's scribble into something that even the client can understand. Art directors are loathe to have people like this working permanently on the staff, lest their presence emphasise how bad an artist the art director actually is, or results in the offer of a permanent job. Possibly the art director's job.

Consultants

Consultants range from a one-person business to a large firm complete with potted plant and tea-lady. Whatever they consult in – marketing, media, creative, etc. – they will do so using jargon that few, if any, people will understand.

You may state that a consultant's true role is to unite the agency team in common hatred, or help prevent the client from discovering how much the agency has blundered.

Consultants have few responsibilities and lots of fun, unless they are advertising people between jobs. However, beware the former ad agency executive consulting for a major international client ostensibly to add marketing or creative 'input', in fact because he knows all the client scandal and is therefore unassailable. Be extremely co-operative with this creature. He (it nearly always is a 'he') might let slip something you can use to your own advantage.

Public Relations People

These fall into two types:

1. Those who work directly for the client, which makes them the agency's enemy since they are both fighting for a larger piece of the budget.

2. Those who work directly for the agency, but would rather work directly for the client.

PR people have two main functions:

– to get media coverage of anything good about their client, and

– to prevent coverage of anything bad about their client.

Whatever the relationship of PR people to the agency, it is best to leave them strictly alone. Unfortunately, it often happens that a PR person working directly for the client produces a plan that runs totally counter to what the agency thinks should be done.

There is only one solution, "research". Few PR people have the facilities to do any 'meaningful' consumer research, and even fewer believe in it. This allows you to say "You've made your point. But we've done the research and we know we're right." If the PR people suddenly appear to know as much about research as you do, send for the nearest planner.

Agencies and PR companies occasionally co-exist in relative harmony, particularly those with a joint financial or business client, or those who have figured out that between them they can persuade the client to increase both advertising and PR budgets.

But it is an uneasy truce. Many PR people are failed journalists or journalists manqué. As such, they are duty bound to hold all advertising people in contempt.

Headhunters

No advertising person will admit to having applied for a job. He or she will always have been headhunted, and then by the hottest headhunter in town.

Headhunters work for agencies and for individuals. Thus they disguise the fact that:

a) an agency is interested in stealing another agency's employee, or needs someone with a particular skill in a hurry;

b) an individual is about to lose his or her job.

If you are approached by a headhunter, never say 'yes' immediately. This takes the fun out of the process for everyone concerned, and headhunters will find it hard to justify their fees. So show some reluctance. Allow them to demonstrate that they have, finally, managed to persuade you to jump ship. They will then be eternally grateful, and think of you the next time an interesting job comes along.

When you need to change jobs, get a friend to approach the headhunter and let it slip that you might be available. When contacted talk of needing a greater challenge; of wanting to realise your full potential; of the next stage in your career plan. They may or may not believe you, but at least you will have observed the proprieties.

Occasionally you will come across a headhunter who is knowledgeable, genuinely sympathetic and honest. Never try to bluff them. Headhunters like these are few and far between in business as a whole, let alone advertising, and should always be encouraged. You never know when you might need them.

THE TRADE PRESS

Like everyone else in advertising, you should:

- decry the trade press as being superficial and uninformed
- read it avidly.

The leading advertising newspaper is big, glossy and printed with plenty of white space. It is very design conscious, which shows in a number of ways:

a) most photographs of agency personnel are taken from somewhere below the subject's left nostril;

b) many photographs of agency personnel are taken in a suitably dramatic location designed to show how modern, tough, fashionable, etc., those agency personnel are;

c) invariably at least three pictures per issue will show an ad person with a potted plant in the background.

You might well ponder on the devotion to style that causes photographers to carry a potted plant with them, wherever they go. But many of these are dictated by ad agency personnel themselves. Not a few may be taken by an agency art director.

If called upon to provide a picture, consider hiding behind the potted plant or providing a shot of yourself setting sail in the single-handed trans-Atlantic yacht race.

By and large, the trade press is read for any one of five main reasons:

* gossip

* to see if a leaked story got in

* to see if the true story was kept out

* acid comments about current and fashionable
  campaigns

* job ads.

Naturally, no-one will ever admit to reading the job ads. But they do. Every week. If only to see how much money they should be earning.

The trade press also becomes the stage for those wonderful agency/client disputes which begin with promises that everything is wonderful, and end with the agency being fired. You must rapidly learn to decipher the seemingly honest comments made by agency and client alike. It might be the only way of discovering that your job will have vanished by next week.

Imagine the scene. The agency (your agency) is relatively peaceful when the latest issue of *Campaign* arrives. There on page one is a report that a client, your agency's major client, is thinking of a move. Not only that, but *Campaign* itself is on the telephone asking for the agency's comments. This is the beginning of a dance as old as advertising itself.

The agency says: We have no comment.

This means: The senior account executive has gone missing.

The agency frantically calls the client seeking a denial.

49

The client says: We are happy with our existing arrangements.

This means: What idiot leaked the fact that we were looking around?

Shortly after this the paper runs a story that the client is reviewing all its advertising. There is a direct quote from both client and agency.

The client says: We have a duty to our shareholders to continually audit all our business operations.

This means: We've just about decided on a replacement.

The agency says: We're proud of our track record with this client and wholeheartedly agree with this review. It gives both of us a chance to build for the future.

This means: Ingrates.

Eventually the client announces that a short list of agencies have been drawn up who will be pitching for the account, present agency included.

The client says: We have a duty to our shareholders to continually monitor the market-place. But we confidently expect our present agency to be with us for years to come.

This means: We've already decided on a replacement. But the marketing director wants to play in a forthcoming Pro Am golf tournament which was arranged by the old agency. And those other agencies who've asked to pitch might just come up with a good idea which the new agency can use.

The agency says: We are confident of keeping the business.

This means: We have decided which of our staff will be let go when we lose the account.

Finally the client announces to the trade press, the appointment of a new agency. This allows three separate quotes to appear:

The client says: Our previous agency did sterling work. But our requirements have evolved to the point that we need the in-depth, specialised agency/client interface that our new agency will provide.

This means: Maybe the new agency will have the sense to listen politely to our chairman's more asinine ideas.

The old agency says: A sad parting of the ways ... total faith in our creative strategy ... in all honesty this account did not prove as profitable as first forecast.

This means: We're already talking to the former client's major rival.

The new agency says: Proud to come on board ... tribute to previous agency ... looking forward to an exciting time ... one of the nation's most dynamic companies ... confidently expect a media spend in excess of £15 million.

This means: We are confident that no-one discovered it was us who leaked the story in the first place.

Awards

The advertising business loves awards and award ceremonies. It is the one time that ad people can admit that they really are in show business.

There is one sure way to win an award: to have been on last year's jury. And then to have given an award to someone on this year's jury.

If you want to be voted on to a jury you must be seen to take advertising seriously. Thus you criticize previous juries for being unintentionally biased and failing to raise professional standards. At the same time, you commend them for doing their best.

You might also cultivate a minor dress idiosyncrasy that will help to earn a reputation for individual eccentricity. (Trainers with a suit no longer works.)

It also helps to develop a reputation for creativity outside the ad business. You might, for example:

a) write a novel that exposes the ad industry in an amusing, non-controversial way

b) be seen at the most media-fashionable art gallery private views

c) go to the theatre (experimental) or ballet (modern) whenever you can.

Note that opera and enjoyable theatre or ballet are only for account executives.

BRIEF HISTORY

Advertising people crave respectability. Not the very successful ones, of course, since they can always buy it, but there are many who wish to be seen as belonging to a profession, not a trade.

This has meant, amongst other things, inventing a new language (see adspeak), and developing a history of advertising as a framework on which to hang the would-be professional banner. The theory appears to be that if advertising can prove it has had a beneficial effect on society then people will have to treat it with a certain respect.

While there might be some small esoteric value in knowing when the first consumer poll was conducted, or why advertising agencies developed, such knowledge is ultimately pointless. After all, you might say, advertising is concerned with the present and the future, not the past. Which is one of those high sounding but ultimately meaningless sentences that will confirm you as a real advertising professional: someone not afraid to obfuscate in order to win the point (or client).

Nonetheless, you should develop your own line in advertising history, if only to annoy those who do take it seriously. You might, for example, mention casually that:

* There is an ancient scrawl in Pompeii advertising the services of a Roman lady of pleasure and that another comment engraved nearby is the first example of a product endorsement.

* Modern advertising effectively began in the USA in the last century, deriving much of its drive, and

modern day approach, from the travelling salesmen who sold bottles of elixir claimed to cure anything from bunions to brewer's droop.

* Radio, far more than television, influenced advertising since soap operas (literally a dramatic series
designed to sell soap) first appeared on US radio, as
did the jingle and the voice-over. You might
practise saying "L-o-o-ove that soap!" in a
Dixieland accent – the slogan that the hero in *The
Hucksters* (the 1940s exposé of Madison Avenue)
developed at the expense of family, friends and
true love. (But he did make agency vice president.)

The point you are making is that advertising is
dedicated to the proposition that nothing succeeds
like excess. It has certainly managed to convince enough
people enough of the time to make it all worthwhile.
Mention, if you like:

- Vance Packard, whose book *The Hidden
Persuaders* and written in the fifties yet again told
the American public how manipulative advertising
was, and first mentioned motivational research
which was the brainchild of :-

- Dr Ernest Dichter, an unreconstructed Freudian,
who claimed to know exactly why people bought
certain things and how they could be subliminally
persuaded to buy yet more things. But who mostly
managed to sell his services to an eager advertising
industry.

Overall, remember that an honest, truthful, legal and
decent history of advertising would destroy overnight

all the mystique the industry has built up over the years.

Advertising may be eminently respectable but the quickest way to lose clients would be to prove it so. Agencies consist of people that clients believe are necessary, but who aren't considered house-trained. Destroy the illusion and you might be out of a job.

For most, the history of advertising is confined to certain campaigns or individual ads that are considered seminal, or not, depending on:

a) your personal point of view

b) the agency you work for

c) whether openly admiring another's work will be good for your own advancement.

You would be best advised merely to comment that all 'great' past advertisements and campaigns are "simply examples of outdated execution coupled with an obvious adherence to essential principles".

Never be drawn on what those essential principles are.

GLOSSARY

Adspeak – A dialect of acronyms and slang designed to impress clients, though those who adspeak the most are invariably the most incompetent.

Agency – A more or less temporary group of people who may or may not believe in advertising, but who do believe in being well paid.

Clients – Those bill-paying people who are:

    a) far sighted, wise and wonderful, or
    b) short sighted, dense and ungrateful,

often both within a single hour.

Consumer – Impossible creature who too often exhibits a mind of his/her own, and who refuses to accept an essentially humble role in the advertising scheme of things.

Account – Agency term for the client and/or product, so named because it pays the agency bills, and because the Agency is made to account for the cost of the advertising, or why the advertising didn't work.

The Brief – Far from brief document explaining the improbable and requiring the impossible.

The Lunch – Neutral ground between expectation and achievement.

Advertisement – Popular form of light entertainment. Never quite as influential as its creators believe.

Copywriter – Would-be poet or novelist, seduced from a garret by the promise of a car and cash, and the chance to see their words in print.

Rough copy – That which awaits the client's own illiterate or cringingly precious contribution.

Body copy – Copy written for the client but aimed at the consumer.

Bastard – a) an awkward (print ad or publication) size; b) the client; c) the consumer.

Art Director – Arbiter of style concerned with the visual aspects of an advertisement or commercial. Or anything.

Art work – Finished ad layout which clients like to scribble on. Anything but a work of art, which is what the art director would prefer to produce if only advertising didn't pay so much.

Scamp – Rough graphic rendition of an ad idea, designed to confuse account executives and clients and stop them from interfering.

Thumbnail – Even rougher rendition, designed to stop the copywriter from interfering.

Logo – Graphic device designed by many and admired by few.

Jingle – Musical rhyme designed to sell a product but which sells its creator's skills.

Slogan – Statement designed to reinforce the client's touching belief in a product, so famous it passes into folk lore ("Beanz Meanz Heinz"), or so fatuous it passes you by ("Building tomorrow, today").

Tag – Words at the end of an ad designed to summarise. Understood by the client, the agency and no-one else.

SFX – Sound effects. Used in commercials to disguise the lack of a good selling idea.

Concept – An ad idea so deliberately vague, as to cause little blame or embarrassment.

Initial concept – That which is hailed as startling, creative, exciting, new.

Final concept – That which can turn out to be flawed, ill-advised and, worst of all, dated.

Contact Report – Essential record of agency/client meeting that has little bearing on what actually occurred. Some clients, fearful of agency bamboozling, produce their own contact reports. These are always as inaccurate and one-sided as the agency variety.

Media – All forms of communication, worshiped by public and advertiser alike.

Deadline – Half an hour ago.

Headline – Claimed by many, written by few.

JICNARS – Readership survey, produced by many and believed by few.

ABC – Official readership figures of a particular periodical, only too believable.

BARB – Official television viewing figures of specific programmes, important to advertising people who fondly believe that those viewers are also watching the commercials adjacent to specific programmes and not making a cup of tea.

Click audience – Viewers/listeners with the habit of changing channels/stations whenever a commercial comes on, not realising it's their duty to watch/listen and buy the product.

Ratings – Points registered for a particular TV programme's popularity but which really only register how many people were in the house when the TV set was turned on. (Called Neilsons in the US.)

Rate card – Official quoted costs of advertising space or time. Like much else in advertising, it has little to do with reality.

RoS (Run of Station) – Non-prime time commercial breaks allocated by TV or radio stations on the basis of, 'We'll fit you in somewhere, don't worry. It'll be worth it.' It never is.

Pitch – The attempt to win an account by parading the agency's best people many of whom the client

may never see again and some of whom may have
been specially hired for the occasion.

Spend – Euphemism for cost.

Total Spend – The estimated cost plus unforeseen
expenses, e.g. a vital creative conference in Tahiti.

Above the Line – Any advertising aimed at the
general public which they find difficult to avoid,
especially commercials, print ads and billboards.

Below the Line – Advertising that uses tightly
controlled delivery techniques, like point of sale
(mini billboards in shops) or direct mail (easy to
ignore by junking).

Advertising Standards Authority – Watchdog for
the industry's code of conduct – all bark and no
bite.

Retail advertising – Form of advertising that most
easily shows up any lack of advertising skill.
Usually the Monday after a weekend sale that
proved a total failure. Primarily concerned with
selling, not with showing how clever the agency is.

Trade and Technical advertising – That which
praises widget-making machines to widget-makers.
Always regarded as being a real grind.

Pharmaceutical advertising – That which promotes
drugs and medical supplies to people who don't
have to pay for them.

Political advertising – A political party's last resort when facing certain electoral defeat. Not apparently bound by the advertising industry's code.

Public Service advertising – That which exhorts people to live cleaner/nicer/safer lives, without any noticeable success.

Business and Financial advertising – That which is greeted with more than usual cynicism by those for whom it's meant.

Advertising – Inspired image-based message without which the world as we know it would collapse.

THE AUTHOR

Nigel Foster's advertising career was distinguished by his inability to take it too seriously.

He achieved brief fame as the first, probably only, person to streak the Women's Advertising and Sales Club of Toronto. To this day, he insists he was trying to prove a product claim.

He admits to a certain pride in having written commercials for the *Sun* and *News of the World* and, along with several others, inventing the Big Stick concept for Wrigleys chewing gum.

He insists that he likes art directors and account executives, but deeply distrusts new clients, especially before lunch.

THE BLUFFER'S GUIDES®

Available at £1.99 and *£2.50) each:

Accountancy
Advertising*
Antiques
Archaeology
Astrology & Fortune Telling
Ballet
Bird Watching
Bluffing
British Class
Chess*
Champagne*
The Classics
Computers
Consultancy
Cricket
Doctoring
The European Community
Finance
The Flight Deck
Golf
The Green Bluffer's Guide
Japan
Jazz
Journalism
Literature
Management
Marketing

Maths
Modern Art
Motoring
Music
The Occult
Opera
Paris
Philosophy
Photography
Poetry
P.R.
Public Speaking
Publishing
Races, The*
Rugby
Secretaries
Seduction
Sex
Science*
Skiing*
Small Business*
Teaching
Theatre
University
Weather Forecasting
Whisky
Wine